The Styer-Fitzgerald Program for Functional Academics

Paraeducator Handbook

Created by

CANDICE STYER, Ph.D.

AND

SUZANNE FITZGERALD, M.Ed.

Published by

Specially Designed
Education Services

The Styer-Fitzgerald Program for Functional Academics
Paraeducator Handbook

Second Edition
First U.S. Edition Published in 2015

SPECIALLY DESIGNED EDUCATION SERVICES
18223 102ND AVE NE
SUITE B
BOTHELL, WA 98011

www.SDESworks.com

ISBN 978-0-9969130-3-4

Cover Design by

hewitt
by design

www.hewittbydesign.com

A big thank you to our editor extraordinaire, Debbie Austin.

Used by permission from The Styer-Fitzgerald Program for Functional Academics,
Secondary Level
©2013 Candice Styer and Suzanne Fitzgerald, Lesson Plans and Data Sheets

Printed by CreateSpace, An Amazon.com Company

Contents

Introduction to the Paraeducator Handbook

This guide is designed to provide you with information about your job requirements and the expectations of you, as a team player, in our special education classroom.

Classroom Mission Statement

_____

_____

_____

_____

_____

_____

_____

_____

_____

Job Expectations

Attendance

Your attendance is vital to the day-to-day functioning of the classroom. When you are absent or late, it impacts both the students and your coworkers. When you need to be away from your job, please try to plan ahead so that appropriate coverage can be arranged.

Professionalism

It is important to have a positive attitude and to act in an age-appropriate manner with students in the special education classroom. Disrespectful or negative behavior is not tolerated. Respect your coworkers' abilities to handle students and situations, and only intervene when asked. When you are working with students be 100% focused. Eliminate personal talk and gossip, and limit the use of cell phones and other personal items to your break times. Treat other staff and students with respect and address situations openly and directly.

Confidentiality

No question is offensive or silly if asked appropriately. If a question is specific to a particular special education student, ask the teacher in private rather than in front of other students or coworkers.

Training

You will be required to assist with teaching students social, leisure, vocational, and academic skills. In addition, you are expected to implement behavior interventions consistently and follow the steps outlined in specific interventions. This manual will help you learn instructional strategies to use in the classroom with the students. You will receive additional training throughout the year.

Data Collection

You will be expected to reliably collect data and record students' progress in each of their individualized programs.

Student Interaction

You are an important role model to the students in your special education classroom. Your job involves many different and equally important duties. In addition to providing academic support, you are also responsible for monitoring and working with students on appropriate behavior and social skills.

We have set high standards and expectations for our special education students. Keep in mind that:

- Having a disability does not give a special education student an excuse for poor behavior.

- You are expected to behave positively and in an age-appropriate manner with your special education students.

- You are expected to monitor students at all times (including during their breaks) to ensure on-task and appropriate behavior.

You are also expected to encourage appropriate interactions and intervene when a student's behavior is inappropriate or harmful. Following are some standards to help guide interactions with students.

- You can practice greetings and simple communication and social skills with your special education students. When you greet a student, be sure that the student gives the appropriate response. The same is true when asking simple questions. It is very common to casually say "good morning" to a student without waiting or listening for a response. Be aware of how you are addressing students and take the time to ensure that they respond appropriately. These skills will serve the students well in the future both socially and vocationally.

- Many special education students do not pick up on the intricacies of social skills from watching their peers. You can facilitate teaching these important skills by modeling appropriate behaviors and also by reinforcing these behaviors as they occur throughout the day.

- You can also create opportunities for your special education students to converse with typically developing peers by showing them how to relate with their peers using symbols and augmentative communication devices. Help facilitate these conversations but do it with the students, not for them.

Additional Expectations

_____

_____

_____

_____

_____

_____

_____

_____

_____

_____

_____

_____

_____

_____

_____

_____

_____

Disability Awareness

It is important to be educated about general disability awareness and etiquette and to learn how to handle difficult situations that may arise. It is also helpful to learn how to work with students who are non-verbal or difficult to understand. The information in this section will be useful in increasing your knowledge about teaching students with more challenging issues or multiple disabilities.

Communication

Remember that there are many ways that special education students communicate with others. Communication can happen through one or more of these ways:

- Verbal
- Tactile
- Sign language
- Modified sign language
- Assistive technology (devices, switches, computers)
- Facial expressions
- Gestures
- Utterances
- Eye gaze
- Modified "yes" or "no"
- Pictures and picture symbols

Steps for Communicating with Non-verbal Students

If you do not understand a special education student, you should not pretend to do so. In such an instance, you can follow these steps:

1. Ask the student to repeat the communication.

2. Say, "I really want to know what you are saying. Please be patient with me and tell me again."

3. If you still do not understand, say, "I still don't understand what you just told me, so I'm going to find another staff person to help me understand."

4. Say, "Thank you for being so patient with me. I really wanted to know what you said."

Here are some things to remember when working with your students:

- Just because someone cannot speak does not mean he or she does not understand.

- Do not talk about students in front of them unless they are included in the conversation. For example, in front of a student **do not** say, "Why does he make that noise?" Instead, say, "I know you are trying to tell us something, so I am going to try to find out what it is. Does anyone know what it means when _____ makes the _____ noise?"

- It is important to include non-verbal students in conversations about their communication. It shows that you care and that you want to understand what they are saying.

Carrying on a conversation with someone who is non-verbal can be difficult. The special education student might not be able to respond to you in a conventional manner. Following are some suggestions for you to try with students that you may be having difficulty communicating with.

- Ask other staff about items or activities a particular student enjoys.

- Ask the student if there are any pictures she can share with you that tell you about her.

- Brainstorm as a team ideas about other topics to discuss with individual students.

- Refer to online websites and search video topics for other tips and ideas. For example, you can refer to the Washington Sensory Disabilities Services website (WSDS—in Washington State) at www.wsdsonline.org.

- If available, obtain a list of suggested conversation topics and age-appropriate step-by-step social scripts.

Tips for Working with Students in Wheelchairs

If you have special education students who are in wheelchairs or who have vision or hearing impairments, you will want to review the following etiquette tips.

- To move a person or take a student who is in a wheelchair to another location, give a warning before moving him or her. Many special education students have heightened startle reflexes and might be easily upset without first knowing what to expect. Following is one strategy for letting the student know what you will be doing.

  1. Tap the student on the shoulder and move to a place where he or she can see and hear you.

  2. Begin with the student's name and say, "___, we are going to go to _____ now, and I'm going to push you there."

  3. Say, "Are you ready?" or "Here we go."

- If a student is not in his or her wheelchair and you need to move the chair, let the student know what you intend to do and where you will move it.

- **Never** hold onto or sit in a student's empty wheelchair—the wheelchair is part of the student's personal space.

Tips for Working with Hearing-Impaired, Visually-Impaired, or Deaf-Blind Students

- If you have a student who is deaf and has an interpreter, be sure to talk to the student and not to the interpreter.

- If you have a student who is blind, talk about what is going on around him or her. For example, "Did you hear the door close? Sally Smith just came into the classroom; she's hanging up her coat."

- As you approach someone who has a dual sensory impairment (deaf-blindness), begin by tapping the person on the shoulder. Then move your hand down the arm until you reach his or her hand; then give your identifier. An identifier is a familiar object that the student has learned to associate with specific people. For example, your identifier might be a ring because your student identifies you by the ring that they always touch when they feel for your hand.

  (Go to www.pathstoliteracy.org/blog/using-personal-identifiers-my-deafblind-son/ for more information.)

  Remember that some students with deaf-blindness often have some hearing and vision. If that is the case, identify yourself verbally or show them your picture so they know who you are.

- When working with students who are deaf-blind, be sure to put your hands underneath their hands rather than grabbing the tops of their hands and manipulating them. This is called "hand-under-hand" and it is less intrusive than grabbing a student by the hand.

- When you walk with a student who is blind or deaf-blind, offer him/her your arm. Watch for and warn them about changes in the terrain, transition strips, doorways, etc. At all times you must be aware of your surroundings so that you can guide them safely.

Handling Inappropriate Behaviors

This section will cover suggestions on how to handle students that act inappropriately in some social situations.

The following example will be helpful if you encounter a situation where a student is trying to get your attention in an inappropriate way. It is important to understand that sometimes our special education students inadvertently invade personal space when they are trying to get attention. It is common for our special education students, who are typically unaware or unsure about how to communicate their feelings, to act inappropriately. For example, a student who wants your attention might give you a hug and not let go or grab your hand or arm without asking permission instead of simply talking to you. If a student enters your personal space, there are ways to respond, depending on the severity of the situation. Following are some suggestions for things to say in such situations.

- "You are in my personal space and you need to back up."

- "This is my space. That is your space. Do not enter my space."

- "You are making me uncomfortable and you need to stop."

- "That is inappropriate. Stop, please."

- If you work in an elementary classroom, you can say, "You didn't ask if you could hug me. You need to ask." Even if a special education student asks first, you need to know that you are not obligated to say "yes" and sometimes, it is good to say "no."

- With an older student you can say something like, "I'm your teacher; you are my student. It's not appropriate for us to hug. You hug people in your family." As students mature, setting appropriate physical boundaries becomes essential. As our students get older and begin spending more time in the community, the issue of safety becomes a reality. As difficult as it may be to refrain from physical reinforcement (i.e., hugs), it is critical to provide these boundaries in order for students to be successful and safe in the community.

Notes

Using Prompts

An important component to providing a cohesive instructional environment is to use prompts or cues in an efficient and effective manner. In addition, the type of prompt or cue that tells students what it is you are asking them to do will differ depending on the skill being taught. For example, in a community setting, the prompt or cue can be the sign at the crosswalk that flashes "Don't Walk." On the other hand, in the classroom during a teaching session, the prompt or cue is the teacher (or you) giving an instruction—for example, "Give me $4.99," or "What time is it?"

It is important to understand not only how to use prompts in different environments but also to know how to determine when the level of prompting should be faded with fewer or no prompts being provided during instruction.

Prompts during Direct Instruction

As stated previously, the type of prompts or cues that you will need to learn to use will vary depending on the skills you are teaching. Following are some pointers when teaching a skill in the classroom (direct instruction).

- Make the prompts clear. Tell special education students exactly what you want them to do. For example, "Give me $4.99."

- Vary the prompts so that students learn that a variety of cues have the same meaning (for example, you can say "$4.99" or "That will be $4.99.")

Next Dollar Strategy

Long-Term Goal:	Short-Term Objective:
Student will use money in the community to purchase items up to $5.00.	Student will count from $0.01 to $5.00 using ones.

Materials: Ten One-Dollar Bills

Notes:

Be sure to stop the student as soon as he or she makes a mistake. Then model the correct response and have him/her try again.

Ask students randomly for less than $1 amounts (.57, .25, etc.) along with even amounts (e.g., $1.00, $2.00, etc.).

If a student is verbal, have him/her count out loud—this is helpful in determining when mistakes are made.

Teach this program in conjunction with Calculator Skills.

Prompt	Correct Response	Correction Procedure	Data
Enter the price into the calculator and say, "Give me _____(e.g., $2.99)."	Student counts out three one-dollar bills for $2.99.	Say, "Stop. Watch me." Model the correct response. Repeat the prompt. If needed, say, "Count with me." Count with the student. Next, say, "Your turn." Have the student count again on his/her own. Reinforce the correct response. For amounts under a dollar say, "Stop. When all you hear is *cents*, you give me a dollar." Repeat the prompt—e.g., "Ninety-nine cents."	**Correct Response:** Praise and circle the corresponding number on the data sheet. **Incorrect Response:** Put a slash through the corresponding number on the data sheet.

Prompts in the Real Environment

When teaching a skill in the community (real environment), you will be using the prompts or cues that occur naturally in that environment. For example, at a street corner, rather than using a verbal prompt of "Stop," you will want to point to the "Walk/Don't Walk" sign and say, "That sign says *Walk*; that means go." Or say, "That sign says *Don't Walk*; that means stop or wait." This technique allows students to respond to the stimuli in the situation (e.g., the green light) rather than to your verbal cue, "Go/Walk." See example lesson plan under Fading Prompts for community-based activity.

Fading Prompts

When you are teaching a skill initially, your prompts should be frequent and concise. After the student begins to learn a skill in the real environment, you need to give him/her the chance to respond on his/her own before providing additional prompts. As students learn a skill, the need for prompting decreases, thus, you can start to "fade" the cues. Fading the cue in the real world, at the right time, is essential to the student being able to use the skill independently. Even when students are becoming fluent with a skill, they may still have difficulty on some of the steps of the activity. When this situation occurs, students may require some prompting but at a reduced level. For example, using the example above, you would say to the student, "That sign says *Walk*, so what do you do?" In this way you are still pointing out the relevant cue (i.e., "The sign says *Walk*"), but you are not telling the student exactly how to respond to the cue.

Community Based Training—Street Crossing

Long Term Goal:	Short Term Objective:
Student will cross streets safely within the community.	Student will cross controlled and uncontrolled streets/ intersections safely.

Materials:	N/A

Notes:
Make a reusable Task Analysis by copying and laminating the reduced size Task Analysis found in the *Reproducible Teaching Materials* binder. Add a hook for a belt or lanyard for easy transport. Use a dry-erase marker to record data and erase after transferring data to final task analysis sheet.

Correction procedures:

- Tell the student to "stop" or "wait," interrupting the behavior chain; this is better than having to go back and correct the behavior later.

- Repeat the S^D. Use the S^D/cue that matches the student's level of skill acquisition (Initial Acquisition or Fading). See "Prompting" section in the *Curriculum* Teaching Guide.

Correction Procedure

	S^D Prompt	Correct Response	Initial Acquisition of Skills when student is first learning	Fading Prompts after student has begun learning	Data
Uncontrolled	At curb	Stops	"Stop/Wait."	"Stop/Wait."	Record the number of prompts per step.
	Waiting	Looks both ways	"You are at the curb (S^D). You need to wait." OR	"You are at the curb (S^D). What do you do?" OR	
	Clear	Crosses the street	"The light is red (S^D).You need to wait."	"The light is red (S^D). What do you do?"	
Controlled	At curb	Stops	"Now that you're waiting (S^D), you need to look in both directions." OR "Now that you're waiting (S^D), you need to look for the light to turn green." "The street is clear (S^D), it is safe to cross now." OR "The light is green (S^D), you need to cross now."	"Now that you're waiting (S^D), what are you looking for?" "The street is clear (S^D). What do you do now?" OR "The light is green (S^D). What do you do now?"	
	Waiting	Looks at light			
	Green light	Crosses the street			
	Red light	Continues to wait			

Notes

_____

_____

_____

_____

_____

_____

_____

_____

_____

_____

_____

_____

_____

_____

_____

_____

_____

_____

_____

_____

_____

_____

_____

_____

Reinforcement

By reinforcing a correct response or behavior you increase the likelihood of the reoccurrence of that behavior. In other words:

BEHAVIOR > SOMETHING "GOOD" HAPPENS > BEHAVIOR IS LIKELY TO REOCCUR
  (*Reinforcement*)

Types of Reinforcement

There are different types of reinforcement. It is important to know which method is best to use as well as when and how to use each type effectively. The following information will be helpful when determining the type of reinforcement to use with particular students.

Verbal Reinforcement

Verbal reinforcement consists of praise or other words of encouragement. For example, "I like how you are staying on task." Or "You really are working hard!"

Physical Reinforcement

There are different levels of physical reinforcement, and each needs to be age appropriate. For example, a hug might be appropriate for an elementary-aged student whereas a pat on the back or a "high five" is more fitting when working with a secondary-aged student.

Tangible Reinforcement

These are items that a student can touch that have reinforcing properties. Examples of tangible reinforcement can include items such as a paycheck, a token, a card with break choices, or a certificate of work well done.

Determining the Type of Reinforcement to Use

The needs of an individual student or the particular lesson being taught often determines the type of reinforcement that will be appropriate. The type of reinforcement is also often a matter of preference of a specific special education student so what works with one student may or may not be effective with another.

You can combine different types of reinforcement. For example, saying "Nice work," while giving a "high five" combines verbal with physical reinforcement. In addition, you can take advantage of activities like break times and build them into your instructional session using them as reinforcement.

Frequency of Reinforcement

The frequency of how often reinforcement occurs depends on where the student is in his or her learning process.

Continuous Reinforcement Schedule
Deliver this method of reinforcement after each and every correct response. Continuous reinforcement is generally used when a student is initially learning a skill.

Intermittent Reinforcement Schedule
Deliver this method of reinforcement after a random number of correct responses. Intermittent reinforcement is generally used when a student has learned a skill but still requires periodic feedback about his or her performance. When you are fading from responding to every behavior to randomly responding, you are using an intermittent reinforcement strategy.

Delivering Reinforcement

Understanding the essential concepts of how to deliver reinforcement is as important as the type of reinforcement you are using. It is vital to the student's learning process that reinforcement be delivered following these guidelines:

- Reinforcement needs to be delivered immediately following the behavior. That way the student is clear about what he/she did to elicit the reinforcement.

- Reinforcement needs to be direct. Clearly state what the student did that resulted in the reinforcement. For example, telling a student "good job" doesn't actually tell the student what "job" caused them to be reinforced. Instead, if the student is told, "You are doing a good job of sitting quietly" then he/she knows that it is the quiet sitting behavior that produced the reinforcement.

- At least when first teaching a skill, the reinforcement should be delivered frequently (i.e., on a continuous schedule). Again, it is important to be aware of when it is suitable to reduce or fade the reinforcement and go to an intermittent schedule. If fading does not happen in a timely way, your student is likely to become satiated with the reinforcement. If this occurs, the reinforcement will no longer hold value and will be ineffective in increasing or maintaining the desired behavior or skill.

Notes

Correction Procedures

Using correction procedures appropriately will facilitate learning and increase the skill levels of your students as effectively as positive reinforcement does. It is important that you understand how to use correction procedures effectively so that your students will learn from their mistakes.

Be sure that you use correction procedures in a way that is educational rather than injurious to a student's self-esteem. Following are some tips on how to phrase a response to an incorrect answer.

Be positive. Avoid saying, "No, that's not right." This type of response is not educational because it does not tell the student what he/she did incorrectly. This response does not take advantage of the teachable moment. To do so, you should say, "The answer is …," or "The clock says …," or "This is 3.99."

Once you've corrected the student by showing him/her the correct response, give him/her a chance to try again.

The following steps illustrate an effective correction procedure:

1. When there is a mistake, say, "Stop" or "Wait," so that the mistake does not continue and become ingrained as part of the skill.

2. Then say, "Watch me." (Model the behavior, such as: "This is $1.20," and count out the amount.)

3. Then say, "Now you try."

4. Then reinforce the correct response. Say, "That's right. That is $1.20."

Lesson Samples of Reinforcement and Correction Procedures

The following diagram illustrates the relationship between prompts, reinforcement, and correction procedures.

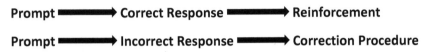

Prompt ➡ Correct Response ➡ Reinforcement

Prompt ➡ Incorrect Response ➡ Correction Procedure

Here are some reminders about how to use reinforcement and correction procedures to teach a skill.

- The response or behavior that previously occurred will be strengthened, if it is followed up immediately with verbal praise (reinforcement).

- Clear and **specific** praise helps a student understand exactly what he or she did correctly. For instance, saying "nice job" lets the student know that he did the right thing, but it does not tell the student what the right thing was. It is better to be specific and say, for example, "Nice job counting out $4.99."

- Be assured that when you use correction procedures appropriately you will not be hurting the student's feelings. Instead, you will be helping them learn.

Reinforcement Sample

The following sample is taken from lessons presented in *The Styer-Fitzgerald Program for Functional Academics* Curriculum. Note the reinforcement for the correct response.

Using reinforcement to teach a skill:

Prompt	Correct Response	Reinforcement
Say, "Give me $4.99."	Student counts out five one-dollar bills.	Say, "Nice job giving me $4.99."

Correction Procedure Sample

The following sample is a lesson presented in *The Styer-Fitzgerald Program for Functional Academics* Curriculum. Note the correction procedure for the incorrect response.

Prompt	Response	Correction Procedure
Say, "Give me $4.99."	Student counts, "One, two, four."	When the student makes the mistake, immediately say, "Stop." Repeat the prompt: "$4.99." Say, "Watch me; one, two, three, four, ninety-nine. Now it's your turn."

The example shows how the teacher stops the student immediately when the mistake is made or when the number three is skipped. Therefore, the student does not learn that four follows two in the sequence. If you do not stop the student at the point of the mistake and he or she keeps counting, the sequence is learned as "one, two, four..." rather than "one, two, three, four..."

After stopping the student, you must clearly demonstrate the correct response. In other words, "Watch me. This is $4.99" as you count out "one, two, three, four..."

It is natural to want to just say "no," give the student the correct answer, and then move on to the next question. However, doing this does not provide the student with the information needed to learn the skill you are trying to teach.

Notes

Data Collection

Data is initially used to evaluate a student's present level of performance and to determine where each student's baseline is in different skill areas. Additional data is collected to track a student's progress and to determine when to move on to the next level of the skill sequence.

Data is also used to analyze whether to make changes to an individual student's programs. For example, if a student has made little or no progress, data would be helpful in determining to stop teaching a skill or to break the skill into easier segments.

The two primary types of data collection described in *The Styer-Fitzgerald Program for Functional Academics* are Discrete Trial and Task Analysis data systems.

The following sections define these format types and show a sample of each type of data sheet.

Discrete Trial—Recording the Percentage Correct

In a discrete trial data system, you will be recording correct responses with circles and incorrect responses with slashes. This will allow you to summarize the data by calculating the overall percentage correct over the total number of trials of instruction for each skill area.

Following is an example of a discrete trial data sheet with sample data. The discrete trial data sheet is the type you will be using when teaching skills such as time-telling or counting coins.

Date:	9/1	9/2	9/3							Correct
	10	10	10	10	10	10	10	10	10	100%
	9	9	9	9	9	9	9	9	9	90%
	8	8	8	8	8	8	8	8	8	80%
	7	7	7	7	7	7	7	7	7	70%
	6	6	6	6	6	6	6	6	6	60%
	5	5	5	5	5	5	5	5	5	50%
	4	4	4	4	4	4	4	4	4	40%
	3	3	3	3	3	3	3	3	3	30%
	2	2	2	2	2	2	2	2	2	20%
	1	1	1	1	1	1	1	1	1	10%

Prompt: "Give me _____."

Task Analysis—Recording the Number of Prompts

The task analysis format is generally used to count the number of prompts per step that are required for a student to perform a particular task or skill. If a student has difficulty with a particular step, you will need to break the task into smaller/simpler steps until the student can perform the task independently.

The task analysis format is the type of data sheet you will use when teaching skills in the community, such as street crossing and grocery shopping. Here is an example of a task analysis sheet with sample data.

Task Analysis		Initials: *AB*	Initials: *AB*	Initials:	Initials:
		Date: *9/1*	Date: *9/4*	Date:	Date:
		Prompts	Prompts	Prompts	Prompts
1	Finds nearest bus stop	//	/		
2	Finds bus number	/	/		
3	Gets on correct bus	//	//		
4	Pays/shows pass	/	/		
5	Finds a seat	//	/		
6	Pulls cord prior to stop	/	/		
7	Exits the bus	/	/		
Total Number of Prompts		10	8		
Bus Stop Location		3rd & Main	B Street		
Final Destination		17th St.	J Street		

Task Analysis—Recording the Type of Prompt

You will encounter this type of data collection system if you are working with the elementary version of *The Styer-Fitzgerald Functional Academics* Curriculum. For example, when teaching a self-help skill to students, you may need to track the type of prompts that you are providing, as opposed to the number of prompts. The decision to use one type of prompt over the other one will be made on a case-by-case basis and depend on the learning style of each individual student.

Student: ___*Bev*___   **Year:** ___*2014*___

Note: This data sheet is designed to track the type of prompt. Use the following key to determine which prompt was used per step. Circle the corresponding letter.

P = Physical   **G** = Gesture   **V** = Verbal   **I** = Independent

Task Analysis	Initials: *SF*	Initials: *CS*	Initials:
	Date: 4/1	Date: 4/2	Date:
	Prompts	Prompts	Prompts
1 Turns on hot/cold water	P G (V) I	P G (V) I	P G V I
2 Picks up soap	P (G) V I	P G (V) I	P G V I
3 Rubs soap on hands	P (G) V I	P G (V) I	P G V I
4 Rinses off soap	P G (V) I	P G V (I)	P G V I
5 Turns off water	P (G) V I	P G (V) I	P G V I
6 Dries hands	(P) G V I	(P) G V I	P G V I
Total Number of Physical Prompts	1	1	
Total Number of Gestural Prompts	3	0	
Total Number of Verbal Prompts	2	4	
Total Number of Independents	0	1	

Accuracy in Data Collection

It is not uncommon to misunderstand what constitutes a prompt and to mark data sheets incorrectly. Training and practice will help you accurately use the two primary systems of collecting data. It is important that you understand that you are not being mean when you are marking a student's response incorrect. The rule for recording a response as correct or incorrect is as follows: If you reinforced the student's initial response, the response is marked as correct. However, if you had to do a correction procedure, the response should be marked as incorrect even if the student went on to respond accurately after having been shown the correct answer.

It is helpful if you put your initials on the days that you collect data. It is also a good idea to note on the data sheets any dates that a special education student's performance might have been affected by illness, lack of sleep, or classroom interruptions.

Notes

Now that you have completed your training you are better prepared to face the challenges of the classroom in which you will work. You have chosen a profession that is both rewarding and arduous. Know that the skills that you possess as a teacher will have a life-long impact on your students. What you do with them every day will change their lives as well as your own.

Appendix A

Pointers for Giving Praise

When you praise one of your special education students, be specific and encourage the response or behavior you want to see again. Here are some suggestions:

"Nice job...

- paying attention."
- following directions."
- listening to instructions."
- acting like an adult."
- speaking like an adult."
- staying on task."
- working hard."

"I like how you...

- are in your own space."
- are sitting like an adult."
- have your hands and feet to yourself."
- are following directions."
- are listening to directions."
- are trying hard."
- are acting like a high school student."
- are *now* using a quieter tone of voice."

Some Other Words of Praise

- "You're doing a much better job working."

- "That's the way to act like an adult."
- "Thank you for working quietly."
- "I'm so glad you made the right choice."

Appendix B

Use the lesson plans for the activities led by the teacher during training.

Activity #5 Lesson Plan: Next-Dollar Strategy

Long-Term Goal:	Short-Term Objective:
Student will use money in the community to purchase items up to $5.00.	Student will count from $0.01 to $5.00 using ones.

Materials: Ten One-Dollar Bills

Notes:

Be sure to stop the student as soon as he or she makes a mistake. Then model the correct response and have him/her try again.

Ask students randomly for less than $1 amounts (.57, .25, etc.) along with even amounts (e.g., $1.00, $2.00, etc.).

If a student is verbal, have him/her count out loud—this is helpful in determining when mistakes are made.

Teach this program in conjunction with Calculator Skills.

Prompt	Correct Response	Correction Procedure	Data
Enter the price into the calculator and say, "Give me _____(e.g., $2.99)."	Student counts out three one-dollar bills for $2.99.	Say, "Stop. Watch me." Model the correct response. Repeat the prompt. If needed, say, "Count with me." Count with the student. Next, say, "Your turn." Have the student count again on his/her own. Reinforce the correct response. For amounts under a dollar say, "Stop. When all you hear is *cents*, you give me a dollar." Repeat the prompt—e.g., "Ninety-nine cents."	**Correct Response:** Praise and circle the corresponding number on the data sheet. **Incorrect Response:** Put a slash through the corresponding number on the data sheet.

Activity #6 Lesson Plan: Telling Analog Time by Quarter Hours

Long-Term Goal: Student will tell time on an analog clock.	Short-Term Objective: Student will tell time by 15-minute, 30-minute, 45-minute, and one-hour increments.

Materials: Analog clock; Three cards with times (only for non-verbal students)

Notes:
For students who have difficulty with telling time by 15, 30, and 45 minutes, break the skill into two sections. First, teach time by the hour and half-hour (Level B1); then add 15 and 45 (Level B2).

Prompt	Correct Response	Correction Procedure	Data
Verbal students: Present the student with the clock and ask, "What time is it?" **Non-verbal students:** Use three cards rather than an analog clock. Say, "Show me ____ (e.g., 9:30)."	**Verbal students:** Student says the correct time. **Non-verbal students:** Student points to the correct time (e.g., 9:30).	Say, "No. It is ____ (e.g., 9:30)." Repeat the prompt (with the same time, 9:30) and ask "What time is it?" (verbal) or "Show me ____." (non-verbal) Reinforce the correct response.	**Correct Response:** Praise and circle the corresponding number on the data sheet. **Incorrect Response:** Put a slash through the corresponding number.

Appendix C

Use the data sheets for the activities led by the teacher during training.

Activity #7 Data Sheet: Next-Dollar Strategy

Student: _____   **Year:** _____

Circle the correct responses and mark a line through incorrect responses. To see a graph of the student's progress, in each column, draw a square around the number that represents the percentage correct; then connect the squares with a line. The "1" through "10" represents both the number of trials on a given day and the percentage correct.

Prompt: "Give me _____." $0.01 – $5.00

Date:

												Correct
10	10	10	10	10	10	10	10	10	10	10	10	100%
9	9	9	9	9	9	9	9	9	9	9	9	90%
8	8	8	8	8	8	8	8	8	8	8	8	80%
7	7	7	7	7	7	7	7	7	7	7	7	70%
6	6	6	6	6	6	6	6	6	6	6	6	60%
5	5	5	5	5	5	5	5	5	5	5	5	50%
4	4	4	4	4	4	4	4	4	4	4	4	40%
3	3	3	3	3	3	3	3	3	3	3	3	30%
2	2	2	2	2	2	2	2	2	2	2	2	20%
1	1	1	1	1	1	1	1	1	1	1	1	10%

Prompt: "Give me _____." $0.01 – $5.00

Date:

												Correct
10	10	10	10	10	10	10	10	10	10	10	10	100%
9	9	9	9	9	9	9	9	9	9	9	9	90%
8	8	8	8	8	8	8	8	8	8	8	8	80%
7	7	7	7	7	7	7	7	7	7	7	7	70%
6	6	6	6	6	6	6	6	6	6	6	6	60%
5	5	5	5	5	5	5	5	5	5	5	5	50%
4	4	4	4	4	4	4	4	4	4	4	4	40%
3	3	3	3	3	3	3	3	3	3	3	3	30%
2	2	2	2	2	2	2	2	2	2	2	2	20%
1	1	1	1	1	1	1	1	1	1	1	1	10%

Activity #7 Data Sheet: Telling Analog Time by Quarter Hours

Student: _____**Year:** _____

Circle the correct responses and mark a line through incorrect responses. To see a graph of the student's progress, in each column, draw a square around the number that represents the percentage correct; then connect the squares with a line. The "1" through "10" represents both the number of trials on a given day and the percentage correct.

Prompt: "What time is it?" or "Show me _____."

Response: Student either says or points to the correct time.

Date:													Correct
	10	10	10	10	10	10	10	10	10	10	10	10	100%
	9	9	9	9	9	9	9	9	9	9	9	9	90%
	8	8	8	8	8	8	8	8	8	8	8	8	80%
	7	7	7	7	7	7	7	7	7	7	7	7	70%
	6	6	6	6	6	6	6	6	6	6	6	6	60%
	5	5	5	5	5	5	5	5	5	5	5	5	50%
	4	4	4	4	4	4	4	4	4	4	4	4	40%
	3	3	3	3	3	3	3	3	3	3	3	3	30%
	2	2	2	2	2	2	2	2	2	2	2	2	20%
	1	1	1	1	1	1	1	1	1	1	1	1	10%

Prompt: "What time is it?" or "Show me _____."

Response: Student either says or points to the correct time.

Date:													Correct
	10	10	10	10	10	10	10	10	10	10	10	10	100%
	9	9	9	9	9	9	9	9	9	9	9	9	90%
	8	8	8	8	8	8	8	8	8	8	8	8	80%
	7	7	7	7	7	7	7	7	7	7	7	7	70%
	6	6	6	6	6	6	6	6	6	6	6	6	60%
	5	5	5	5	5	5	5	5	5	5	5	5	50%
	4	4	4	4	4	4	4	4	4	4	4	4	40%
	3	3	3	3	3	3	3	3	3	3	3	3	30%
	2	2	2	2	2	2	2	2	2	2	2	2	20%
	1	1	1	1	1	1	1	1	1	1	1	1	10%

Activity #7 Task Analysis: Bus Riding (Number of Prompts)

Student: _____**Year:** _____

	Task Analysis	Initials: Date: Prompts	Initials: Date: Prompts	Initials: Date: Prompts	Initials: Date: Prompts	Initials: Date: Prompts
1	Finds nearest bus stop					
2	Finds bus number					
3	Gets on correct bus					
4	Pays/shows pass					
5	Finds a seat					
6	Pulls cord prior to stop					
7	Exits the bus					
	Total Number of Prompts					
	Bus Stop Location					
	Final Destination					

Activity #7 Task Analysis: Hand Washing (Type of Prompts)

Student: _____**Year:** _____

Note: This data sheet is designed to track the type of prompt. Use the following key to determine which prompt was used per step. Circle the corresponding letter.

P = Physical   **G** = Gesture   **V** = Verbal   **I** = Independent

	Task Analysis	Initials: Date: Prompts	Initials: Date: Prompts	Initials: Date: Prompts	Initials: Date: Prompts	Initials: Date: Prompts
1	Turns on hot/cold water	P G V I	P G V I	P G V I	P G V I	P G V I
2	Picks up soap	P G V I	P G V I	P G V I	P G V I	P G V I
3	Rubs soap on hands	P G V I	P G V I	P G V I	P G V I	P G V I
4	Rinses off soap	P G V I	P G V I	P G V I	P G V I	P G V I
5	Turns off water	P G V I	P G V I	P G V I	P G V I	P G V I
6	Dries hands	P G V I	P G V I	P G V I	P G V I	P G V I
	Total Number of Physical Prompts					
	Total Number of Gestural Prompts					
	Total Number of Verbal Prompts					
	Total Number of Independents					

Made in the USA
Middletown, DE
10 September 2023

37955293R00027